MORE Land Buying Tips from the Pros

How to Buy Rural Real Estate

Written & Compiled by Pat Porter

Copyright 2017 by Pat Porter

Published by RecLand Realty, LLC Monroe, LA 71201

All rights reserved. No part of this publication may be reproduced, stored in a retrieval system or transmitted in any form or by any means – electronic, mechanical, digital, photocopy, recording or any other – except for brief quotations in printed reviews, without the prior permission of the publisher.

Why We Write These Land Books

You know, the real estate category is very small within the overall Amazon book universe. And the rural real estate (land) niche is just a tiny speck tucked away in a corner of that category. I know I'm not going to be writing the next Harry Potter epic and selling millions of copies or be on some national bestseller list. And I can live with that.

My goal with these books – this will be the sixth one – has been to provide a source for good, easy-to-read, common-sense information to support our industry. Land brokerage is a multi-billion dollar per year industry here in the United States. More and more people want to own a slice of heaven. I want to help them do it and to contribute all I can in support of the great industry that has supported me. These books are a humble attempt to do just that.

So read, enjoy, think, learn, and pass it along.

Please check out all our land-related books at my Amazon Author Page.

Our RecLand Talks video blog has lots of specific information about land management, hunting and the outdoors, and who we are at RecLand. Check it out at www.RecLandTalks.com. Take a look at our other blog at www.LandInfoSite.com.

— Pat Porter

Contents

List of Contributors 9

Introduction 10

Chapter 1 - How to Evaluate Land You Plan to Build On 12

    Ask yourself the following questions: 13

        1.   How far am I willing to commute to work? 13

        2.   What do I like to do for fun? 13

        3.   Does the area accommodate any specialized needs or services myself or a family member requires? 14

        4.   What is the proximity to family and friends? 14

    Determine if your experienced land agent can answer the following questions: 15

        1.   Is the land definitely buildable? 15

        2.   Have state, federal, or environmental regulations 15

        3.   Has a soil test been performed? 15

        4.   Is the land in a flood zone? 16

        5.   Is there access to utilities? 16

        6.   What is the property zoned 16

        7.   How is the land accessed? 16

Chapter 2 - Pitfalls for Buyers in Real Estate Closings 18

    1.   Lack of complete or full information. 19

    2.   Relying on unconfirmed or unwritten information 20

    3.   Good legal description of the property 20

    4.   Lack of access. 21

    5.   Lack of survey 22

Chapter 3 - Access Scenarios to Consider 25

    1.   Existing legal access to a public road. 26

        a.   Check to see that what the document 29

      b. Be sure the easement is well-identified in that document. 29

      c. I would recommend that clear language 29

   2. No existing legal access. But you can acquire it. 30

   3. No existing legal access, and the adjoining landowners will not cooperate in granting you one. 31

      a. Don't buy the property. 32

      b. Get a legal opinion regarding your rights to sue for access. 32

      c. Buy the property and try to work it out later. 33

   4. A physical road or trail, but not a deeded access. 34

Chapter 4 - Buying Land in the American West 37

  Valuation...38

  Water Rights 39

   1. Examine the historical usage 40

   2. Understand the priority dates 40

   3. Research the water right values 40

  Public Lands 40

Chapter 5 - The Basics of Financing Unimproved Land.............................44

  Here are a few things I tell my customers 44

   1. Know where you stand financially. 44

   2. Meet with your banker prior to making an offer to purchase land. 44

   3. Research the land you are looking to purchase as well as similar types of property. 45

   4. Be realistic and provide room for the unknown. 45

   5. Know what you can afford. 46

   6. Research the programs that might be available for the land you are purchasing. 46

  Here are a few other things to be keep in mind when you are financing a land purchase...47

1. Understand that there will be additional out-of-pocket costs ..47

2. There will be costs for the upkeep and maintenance of your new property. 48

3. Talk to your CPA or tax professional about your land................48

Chapter 6 - Should You Get a Survey? 50

Some general information regarding the profession of surveying: 50

1. It's been said that surveying is one of mankind's oldest professions.................50

2. Surveyors are required to have a working knowledge of many subjects 51

3. A number of famous men were some of the first surveyors in our nation 51

4. Surveyors must use more than just scientific data 51

Let's now take a look at some reasons why you should consider surveying your next tract 53

1. A survey confirms a description on the ground of the property that is in the public records. 53

2. A survey will identify any encroachments. 53

3. A survey will identify any easements 54

4. A survey will confirm legal access. 54

5. A survey is necessary if you plan to develop and accurately divide a tract. 54

6. You will need a land survey to get the full benefits of your title policy coverage. 55

7. Old surveys are likely not as accurate as new surveys...............55

8. A survey will shed light on any existing fences. 56

9. Get a survey if you plan to build on the tract. 57

10. Get a survey to document what is on the ground. 57

11. Get a survey if you want to buy by the acre. 58

Here are a few general reasons I may elect to pass on the survey:........59

- 1. There was a recent survey. 59
- 2. It's a well-marked timberland tract 59
- 3. The property adjoins state or federal land. 60
- 4. The aerial imagery maps out to the correct acreage. 60

Let me give you a few tips to help you get the most out of your survey: 60

- 1. Always get a plat. 60
- 2. Identify any existing monuments on the tract ahead of time. ...61
- 3. Have the surveyor mark some additional points along long boundary lines. 61
- 4. Mark the lines yourself. 62
- 5. Try to use the same surveyor if possible. 62

Wrapping It All Up 64

Other land and real estate books by Pat Porter: 65

"How to Sell Your Land Faster – Proven Ways to Improve the Value & Desirability of Rural Land" 65

"The Stuff the Best Land Agents Do: And You Should Do Them, Too!" 65

"Land Buying Tips from the Pros – How to Buy Rural Real Estate" ...66

"Land Mines: Lessons to Keep Your Rural Real Estate Deals from Blowing Up" 66

"Dumb Questions: Avoid Asking These Questions When You Are Buying Rural Real Estate" 66

Bonus Chapter 67

Due Diligence – Some Additional Items to Check before Buying Rural Land 67

The Purchase Contract 67

Existing Easements & Leases 68

Wetlands 70

Environmental Issues 70

Timber Markets...71

Title, Mineral and Groundwater Checks 71

Flood Plains and Access to River Tracts 72

List of Contributors

Below is a list of the land pros who've contributed to this book. Their professional and personal information is at the end of each of their chapters.

While we are often competitors in the land business, we typically work well with one another, support each other and respect each other's knowledge and businesses. We frequently share information and work together in land transactions. Please feel free to contact any of these people to inquire regarding their services or ask any questions about their chapter.

Jennifer Beecher – Communications Manager for the LANDFLIP Network in Madison, Georgia and Land Agent with Mossy Oak Properties Coastal Land and Real Estate in St. Marys, Georgia.

Jarrod Sellar – Senior Loan Office for Louisiana Land Bank, ACA in Monroe, Louisiana.

Ed Roberson – Ranch Broker, Mirr Ranch Group in Denver, Colorado.

Kirby O. Price – Attorney, North Delta Title Company in Monroe, Louisiana.

Pat Porter – Owner/Broker of RecLand Realty, LLC in Monroe, Louisiana.

Introduction

If you get good information, you can make a good decision. This book will give you some good information about many different aspects of buying rural land. That was the goal.

I called some top land professionals and asked them to write a chapter about a specific subject that would help people in their land buying process. I, too, added a chapter. The results provided a no-fluff resource that addresses many of the questions land buyers have.

There is no theory here. This information comes from decades of combined experience and hundreds of millions of dollars of combined land transactions from the contributors. The information offered here has been fleshed out in the real world of timberland, farm land, recreational properties, development tracts, and closing tables where people have bought and sold thousands of acres of rural real estate.

Each writer puts forth his information from their own unique prospective and in their own style.

The book is written in such a way that you can skip around from chapter to chapter and get good information about certain subjects you have interest in. I'd recommend, however, that you read it straight through. Sure, you may find yourself reading about a type of land you're not currently pursuing. But you'll gain a deeper overall understanding of how to approach rural real estate – like these folks do - and this will likely cause you to look at your next purchase in a different way. You'll pick up on common threads that each writer mentions that seem to apply across all or most potential land buys.

Well, let's get on with. Take a look at the first chapter of "Land Buying Tips from the Pros."

****

WAIT! That was the introduction for the first "Land Buying Tips from the Pros" book. It summed things up so well that I didn't see any need to change it too much.

That book is very popular, too! So popular that I decided to publish "MORE Land Buying Tips from the Pros" from a different group of land professionals. You'll still get a no-fluff resource, but it'll have a few new subjects.

Well, let's get on with it. Dive into the first chapter of "MORE Land Buying Tips from the Pros."

Chapter 1 - How to Evaluate Land You Plan to Build On

By Jennifer Beecher – Professional Land Agent & Communications Manager at the LANDFLIP Network

"Take me home, country roads" isn't just a line from John Denver's hit song anymore. As more residents of big cities across America grow tired of the rat race, country living is becoming quite desirable. With the rising ability to work from home, people are seeking their own little slice of heaven in the country where they can pursue a self-sustaining lifestyle, raise their families, and maybe even live off the land.

You might have read some of the informative articles that have been published on www.LANDTHINK.com that address common situations land buyers encounter when purchasing farmland, timberland, or other large acreage tracts for investment, hunting, and recreation. This chapter, however, is geared toward land buyers who are embarking on a journey to locate and purchase a smaller parcel of land (or lot) on which to build their future dream home.

Aside from the usual considerations, such as knowing your price range, choosing a buyer's agent, determining potential resale value, and conducting due diligence, the evaluation process for land you intend to build on comes with a different set of considerations than do other types of land purchases. I'll cover some of the not-so-obvious as well as emotional aspects involved in purchasing land that buyers should keep in mind when beginning their search for the perfect piece of property for their future home, be it a primary residence or a second home.

If you're just beginning your search for a homesite on land listing sites such as www.LOTFLIP.com, LANDFLIP's complementary site devoted to land for sale under 20 acres, or if you've wisely secured the services of an experienced land agent, keep these tips in mind when looking for a future building site.

Never purchase sight unseen. Buying land to build on is an emotional decision. Being a REALTOR® and land agent since 2005, I've been involved in numerous real estate transactions where buyers purchased a future homesite without ever stepping foot on the land. Walk each parcel pin to pin (that's corner to corner!), and involve all members of the family. Reconsider going to contract without the presence of a spouse, partner, or other decision maker. Buying land is one of the biggest decisions you'll make in your lifetime. It should never be purchased on impulse.

Location, location, location. We've all heard it, but where you decide to build your home will greatly influence the lives of you and your family.

Ask yourself the following questions:

1. How far am I willing to commute to work? If you're not retired, and don't have the luxury of working from home, take into consideration how much of your day will be spent on the road. Even if gas prices are low, commuting could take a toll on your time and your wallet.

2. What do I like to do for fun? This is a question I always like to ask my clients who are unfamiliar with the area in which they are inquiring about purchasing a homesite. Make sure the area you choose will offer you the opportunity to

participate in the types of recreational activities that you and your family enjoy.

3. Does the area accommodate any specialized needs or services myself or a family member requires? I got started in the real estate business selling homesites for major developers, and I've seen this factor be the deal-breaker on more than one occasion. Medical, educational, and other special needs must be addressed; otherwise, building in the location – even if everything else about it is perfect – would be completely impractical.

4. What is the proximity to family and friends? Life is filled with inevitable and momentous events like births, graduations, and weddings. Factor in the distance you're putting between you and the most important people in your life.

Envision your dream homestead. Take time to write down property characteristics you want in a homesite and present this list to your land agent. It's important for your agent to know what you can and can't live without. How much property do you need to build a home the size that you desire? Do you want close neighbors or total seclusion? Do you desire waterfront property? Do you want rolling or flat terrain? Do you plan to have a garden, orchard, or animals? Do you like trees or streams? Is there room for a pool? Knowing exactly what you want will not only ensure that the property meets your goals and objectives, it will also be significant in determining the building envelope for your future home.

Invite your builder along to evaluate your top selections. A homebuilder can help determine the building envelope and even suggest home plans that are best suited for the topography of the land. I've sold waterfront lots on Lake Guntersville in Alabama that many clients, upon first look at the drastic elevation, would have thought it to be impossible to build upon. With the guidance of an experienced, reputable homebuilder, buyers are capable of building a beautiful home on land that, at first glance, can appear to be adverse terrain.

Inquire regarding property regulations. If the property is in a subdivision, is there an Architectural Review Board? What are the Covenants and Restrictions? Reading through a full, up-to-date copy of a subdivision's Covenants and Restrictions can be a daunting task, but it's very important that you have a clear understanding of the neighborhood rules. If you have any questions, write them down and consult a real estate attorney. Also, remember to ask about the annual Homeowners' Association (HOA) dues, and what you receive in return for payment of your dues. If the community is gated and the roads are not maintained by the county, major developers will sometimes have an escrow account devoted to repaving or repair of roads.

This list of things to keep in mind when buying a future homesite is not intended to be comprehensive. Buying land is a complex transaction, and there is a lot you need to know.

Determine if your experienced land agent can answer the following questions:

1. Is the land definitely buildable? Has the lot has passed a percolation test? Is a septic system allowed, or does the neighborhood tie into a public water and sewer system?

2. Have state, federal, or environmental regulations (regarding wetlands, endangered species, etc.) that might affect your ability to build been considered?

3. Has a soil test been performed? Soil analysis is important in determining the type of home foundation best suitable for the soil type. It is usually required for building permits, but you or your land agent can have one performed to alert you

to any possible hazards to your future home or land investment.

4. Is the land in a flood zone? What is the approximate cost of flood insurance in the area? Usually, residents of private gated communities cannot apply to the Federal Emergency Management Association (FEMA) for cleanup after a major disaster like a hurricane. You can find useful information about flood plains, etc. at https://www.fema.gov/.

5. Is there access to utilities? If buying rural acreage, the cost to run power to your home could be a big part of your budget, so you want to secure an estimate before purchasing. If the lot is in a neighborhood, are the infrastructure and amenities in place? If all amenities are not complete, is the project bonded by the developer to ensure that all promises made by the developer to buyers will be completed within a reasonable timeframe? This is a smart question to ask if you're planning on the future enjoyment of a subdivision's planned amenities like a golf course, marina, community dock, or swimming pool.

6. What is the property zoned, if the homesite you're considering is not located in a platted subdivision? What are the property taxes?

7. How is the land accessed? Public road? Private road? Easement? Your land agent can help you make this determination and avoid any potential confusion or complication.

Finding the homesite that best suits your needs can take time and perseverance, but having an agent to guide you through every step of the buying process will help ensure that your decision will ultimately be one that brings years of happiness and enjoyment to your entire family.

About the Author

Born and raised in South Georgia, Jennifer Beecher has extensive knowledge of the surrounding areas, which is a valuable resource for her clients. She obtained her real estate license in 2005 and has worked for two premier land developers: Bluegreen Communities and Redstone Properties. Jennifer has also worked with K. Hovnanian Homes, a national homebuilder, as a new home Sales Consultant. From 2010-2012, she was affiliated with Innovative Land Solutions in Brunswick, Georgia, and in early 2013 she joined Mossy Oak Properties Coastal Land and Real Estate in St. Marys, Georgia. Jennifer has participated in a variety of real estate transactions, but she specializes in assisting buyers and sellers by analyzing and negotiating the sale or purchase of land all over South Georgia. In 2011, she joined the team at www.LANDFLIP.com and www.LANDTHINK.com as Communications Manager. Jennifer graduated from Georgia Southern University in 2003 with a B.S. degree in Public Relations. Jennifer can be reached by email at jbeecher@mossyoakproperties.com.

Chapter 2 - Pitfalls for Buyers in Real Estate Closings

By Kirby Price – Attorney at North Delta Title Company

In my years (which seem far too many!) of handling real estate transactions, I have witnessed several common "pitfalls" to closings. The basic goal of all parties to a real estate transaction is essentially the same: a smooth and efficient transfer of title to property.

For the seller, the ultimate goal is the receipt of the proceeds from the sale (getting the money!). For the buyer, the goal is obtaining ownership of the property they want to acquire without complications or clouds on the title. For other parties to the transactions such as attorneys, surveyors, lenders, insurance agents, and Realtors, the goal is payment for their services, happy clients, and the personal satisfaction of knowing their clients have obtained their objective in the transaction and are pleased with the services each party provided. Everyone wants a successful closing!

In thinking back on issues that have hindered a successful closing, several things jump out as being reasons for the closing to not be as smooth or successful as one would like. In no particular order, they include the following:

1. Lack of complete or full information.

2. Reliance on unconfirmed or unwritten information.

3. Lack of a good legal description of the property.

4. Lack of access.

5. Lack of survey.

Real estate transactions can fairly easily be divided into two basic categories: residential and commercial. Residential transactions are just that: for personal residences. Commercial transactions can include buildings and unimproved, open land. While the basic issues are present in both residential and commercial transactions, the absence of the above items creates, in my opinion, more severe complications in commercial transactions. For that reason, the remainder of this brief chapter will center on commercial transactions, primarily involving larger land tracts. Let's look at each of those items a little closer.

1. Lack of complete or full information. In order to successfully begin and conclude the transaction, full and complete information, including the full legal names of the buyer and seller and the addresses for tax purposes, is necessary. If a legal entity is used (LLC, Corporation, etc.) rather than individuals, as the buyer, as the seller, or as both, the person or persons representing the legal entity must be designated and duly authorized in writing to be the representative. If the seller or buyer is an individual and cannot be present at the closing, then a written power of attorney acceptable to the lender and closing agent will be needed. In any event, the absence of information about the legal representative of the selling or buying legal entity, and their authority to act, or the inability of the individual buyer or seller to be physically present at closing, will in most cases cause a delay in closing.

Authority to sign on behalf of an entity and/or another individual in a real estate transaction is a serious responsibility. The documents granting that responsibility can vary from state to state, though they often must include specific language and can require specific procedures for signing by the involved parties in order for the sale to be valid. It's wise, therefore, to send a copy of this document to the closing attorney or title company for a review well in advance of the scheduled closing to be sure it is suitable for that transaction in that state.

2. Relying on unconfirmed or unwritten information. This item dovetails with item 1, but also includes a failure to verify information, or a reduction of the verification to writing. It also dovetails with the remaining items discussed below. Each real estate transaction requires many specific items of information. These are like pieces of a puzzle which are supposed to all come together upon the completion of the puzzle – a successful closing. For this successful closing to occur, each piece of the puzzle needs to be verified – from the more obvious ones, like verification that the seller actually owns the property being bought by the buyer, and that the mortgage currently on the property is the one being paid off and cancelled, to the more mundane items, such as correct mailing addresses and the names of spouses and/or previous spouses, as applicable, for the buyer and seller.

3. Good legal description of the property. I began by stating that the list of pitfalls was in no particular order. If they were, this one would be at the top of the list. The absence of a good legal description of the property the seller wants to sell and the buyer wants to buy complicates the closing process. And if this is not successfully addressed, it can result in a closing no party is pleased with.

So what is a good legal description? Simply put, it is an exact and verifiable description of the property. Property is often described as going to the edge of a certain road, or to a particular fence corner, or to a certain oak tree, or to the high bank of a creek. While those points were likely obvious to the people when the property was originally described, over time those points can change – and probably have!

A good legal description is one which allows any third party to clearly define what is being bought or sold. And since all title and ownership of property is determined by the information filed in the clerk of court records of all local governments, it is imperative, in order for a merchantable title to exist, that an examination of the records reflect the legal description of the property. In summary, a buyer needs to know with certainty what is being sold and bought. The lender, if one is used, needs to know that the property, which likely provides the collateral for its loan, is clearly defined and insured. This must be more than what someone thinks they own; it must be what is definitively provided in the public records. The "records" are the basis of all real estate ownership and transfers.

4. Lack of access. Access to a public road is essential for the full use of property by the owner. It is also necessary to maximize the value of the property for the seller, buyer, and lender. Access is not only the "actual ability" to connect by vehicular means to a road, street, or highway maintained by a public body. Access needs to also be a legal access. A legal access is one that is provided in one of two ways:

   a. By the property fronting directly adjacent to a public road OR

   b. Not lying adjacent to a public road but is provided for in a written and duly filed document creating the right of access to a public road.

> The written right of access needs to also define the obligations for each party for maintenance of the access. The document providing access needs to clearly define the access points and dimensions as well as other terms such as duration, time, maintenance, and restrictions.

States vary regarding the specific language required to fully define a legal access. Be sure to talk with your real estate attorney if you question the legal access to a property you are buying.

5. Lack of survey. Until several years ago, surveys were important elements in all real estate transactions. As a result of the creativity and marketing skills of title insurers, surveys for most residential transactions are not obtained nearly as much. In commercial transactions (like larger land tracts), they are of particular importance.

   Although a survey often involves a significant financial element of the transaction, it often provides crucial information about the physical condition of the property being purchased by a buyer and the collateral offered to a lender. Such things as access, encroachments, location of improvements, and evidence of actual physical possession of the property by people/parties other than the record owner are important factors to a buyer and the lender. These factors help determine the suitability of the property for its planned use by the buyer and its value to both the buyer and the lender.

   I would suggest giving serious consideration to obtaining a boundary survey for any purchase you are about to make. The cost of the survey can be negotiated with the seller as part of the deal. The cost of the survey today may well be much cheaper than the cost of the problems you may have to resolve later.

You can see that there is a common thread flowing through this brief discussion about the potential pitfalls of closings: it is the attention to details that makes the difference. Addressing all the details, regardless of how minor they may appear, and doing so sooner rather than later, can save you money, time, and disappointment.

The best way to address the details is at the very beginning in the purchase agreement. A detailed purchase agreement provides the road map to the closing table. The more accurate the details are that are provided from the beginning in the purchase agreement, the more likely it is that a smooth and orderly transaction will proceed. Such details help result in a transaction which is not delayed due preventable, unexpected surprises. For sure, there often occur unexpected surprises in any transaction that couldn't have necessarily been prevented in the purchase agreement. But tying down details early on will help prevent many good faith misunderstandings and delays at the last minute when you are ready to close.

About the Author

Kirby O. Price has resided in Monroe, Louisiana for more than 40 years. He received a Bachelor of Science degree from the University of Louisiana at Monroe in 1971 and earned his MBA from ULM in 1972. He graduated in 1978 from the Paul M. Hebert School of Law at Louisiana State University, earning a Juris Doctorate. He has practiced law in Monroe since 1978, focusing on business transactions and real estate law.

Mr. Price's practice includes representation of both buyers and sellers, as well as lenders and borrowers, in various secured and unsecured transactions, as well as contractual matters such as leases, condominiums, and the formation of legal entities. Mr. Price has received an AV Preeminent peer rating through Martindale-Hubbell. He is a member of the American Bar Association, the Louisiana State Bar Association and the Fourth District Bar Association. He is certified as a real estate instructor by the Louisiana Board of Realtors. He can be reached at North Delta Title Company in Monroe, Louisiana at https://ndtc.nettechdata.com/.

Chapter 3 - Access Scenarios to Consider

By Pat Porter – Broker/Owner, RecLand Realty, LLC

I wrote a research paper on Robert Frost's "The Road Not Taken" when I was in the tenth grade. While this chapter is not a formal research paper, I could have called it "The Road Not There" and wouldn't have been off point.

My work as a land broker puts me on a collision course with access issues almost weekly. Quite often, we have land tracts with the major hurdle being "the road not there." There is just no legal, deeded access to connect the property to a public road. Depending on the type of property, this can result in the tract being very difficult to sell. Understanding the access to a tract you are thinking about buying should be in the top three items on your due diligence list.

"But, Pat, people can't keep me from accessing my land, can they?" Well, in a word...yes.

States have different laws regarding access to a "landlocked" property. And even within a state, there can be different types of access and specifics regarding how access is or is not acquired, granted, and even lost. To be sure, it can get complicated depending on where you are, the specific situation you have, and how you can go about remedying it. And even if the laws are in your favor for obtaining the right to access a currently landlocked tract, time-consuming and expensive processes must be often undertaken before that right can be fully enjoyed.

Let's look at a few scenarios regarding access and what we can learn to be sure we have both eyes open when buying land.

1. Existing legal access to a public road. This is simply when the legal boundary of a property lies adjacent to the boundary of the public roadway, and there are no gaps between those boundaries. Said another way: the property "fronts" a public road.

   This is the situation for most homes in the town where you live. The lot your home is situated on at 131 Elm Street touches the street right of way, and you have unrestricted ingress and egress from your private lot to the public road. The right of way is not the edge of the pavement. It will likely extend beyond that on both sides to include any shoulder and possibly the ditches. Public right of ways typically have a defined width (examples: 40 feet, 60 feet, and even much wider on some highways).

   This is pretty straight forward. But let me ask you this: How do you know – I mean KNOW – your property line actually bounds the public right of way in sufficient distance to actually provide a legal access? That's right…you just assume! Or you are making a pretty well-reasoned assessment.

   The only way to really know, though, is with a boundary survey. Kirby Price, an attorney with a title company here in Monroe, Louisiana, briefly mentions this in his chapter on "pitfalls". He discussed how few surveys are now done on residential sales as compared to days passed and the problems that can be prevented by having a survey done.

   Here's a recent example. One of my residential agents with another company I'm a part owner in recently had a contract on a home she listed in our area. The buyer, represented by another broker, had a boundary survey performed since the seller was excluding a large, custom barn and about ¼ of an acre from the sale. The survey, originally needed to carve the homesite away from the barn, actually uncovered a potentially large issue. It was a surprise to everyone when the survey revealed that the driveway to the house actually crossed the neighbor's property before connecting to the street.

Everyone assumed the concrete driveway that went from the garage out to the street was part of our seller's property. Most of it was. But a lot of it wasn't. The seller had to make last minute arrangements to secure an unbroken access to the street from the property he was selling.

You just don't know until you know. It's usually a lower-risk assumption when dealing with properties on well-established streets and roads in neighborhoods, towns, or cities. But it can be less of a sure thing when dealing with rural property or when the road is not improved and can move over time (example: timber company roads). Be sure the access you are counting on is verified. Talk to your land agent and attorney to get guidance on how to verify this if you are concerned.

Remember at the beginning of this scenario I wrote "…no gaps between those boundaries"? I meant that. No gaps!

A couple years ago, I was part of a group that bought a large, rural tract for a development project. It had over ¼ mile frontage on a public road – or so I thought. I was just a little uncertain, so I had a boundary survey performed before the closing to verify the tract indeed laid adjacent to that road.

The survey revealed it laid adjacent to a 15-foot-wide strip between the edge of the road and our property line. This would be that "gap" I referred to. An inch is a mile when it comes to being adjacent versus not being adjacent. The road right of way was not well defined in the public records. This 15 feet, however, was dedicated for public utilities along that public road, according to documents in the public records, so I felt comfortable we had a legal access to the right of way. Remember Kirby Price, my attorney friend and veteran of thousands of real estate closings? He wasn't so comfortable. In fact, he pointed this potential gap out to me and said he'd recommend checking into it more before we closed. But the lender was comfortable. I was somewhat confident. We closed.

Long story short…that gap was indeed a problem…and then it wasn't…then it was again…and then it finally wasn't. The fact that it was there, and that the roadway language was unclear, caused some in the area who had oversight with our subdivision approval to delay that approval for over a year. It took that long before it could be determined to their satisfaction that we did have a legal access to the roadway that was beyond the 15-foot utility servitude area. Title insurance was bought to cover any unknown future disputes. The year-long delay, attorney fees, another survey, and additional title insurance was expensive. The access is settled now, but the concern was that small gap.

Let's look at another way to have legal access.

You can have legal access to a public road even if the property is not adjacent to the road. If the current seller has a "deeded access" that grants a specific route from his tract to the public road, or can acquire this granted access before he sells the property to you, you are good to go. Just have your attorney confirm a few things:

a. Check to see that what the document grants (what we are calling "deeded access" here for simplicity) is truly an acceptable grant or conveyance of that access in perpetuity. That means that it "runs with the land", so to speak, and is permanent. So regardless of who may buy or sell either your tract or the tract(s) the access crosses over, the access will remain in place. It is in place permanently because it's in favor of your land tract and any future owner, heir, successor, etc., not just you personally. (Side note: For you legal experts out there, I know some situations can cause that access to be dissolved even if originally established as a perpetual easement, but we're not going to wander into those weeds here.) The point is to be sure the document you are relying on for legal access is what you need for it to be permanent and to have it covered by a title policy.

b. Be sure the easement is well-identified in that document. This is where your attorney, lender, or both may tell you to have it surveyed – if it hasn't been – so it can be tied to a verifiable geographic location. Roads can move. Rural, timberland roads can definitely move. Be sure to nail down that access route with specific, detailed language, as well as a detailed plat map showing the route from the public road to a point touching your boundary line.

c. I would recommend that clear language about who maintains the access road and to what degree is spelled out. Roads require maintenance. Who's going to do it and to what standards? Who can be held liable if someone gets hurt or has property damaged on that road? Remember, you may have a legal right to use a road, or build a road, but it's still on someone else's property if you only have a deeded easement.

2. **No existing legal access. But you can acquire it.** Maybe the tract has a physical road or trail that will join a public road, or maybe it doesn't. In either case, the road, or place where a road would feasibly be located, is across someone else's property.

   We deal with this scenario often. The sale of the landlocked tract requires some work to acquire a written authorization to traverse the land between the tract and the road. The owner(s) of that property must grant the right of ingress, egress, and any servitudes or easements needed for potential utilities. The written grant of this right is often referred to as deeded access. It is called this because a permanent servitude (the word "easement" is used in most states) must be granted in some type of document that is recognized in your state as a legal grant of those rights.

   We secure these easements routinely from timber companies in our region. It's usually a simple but not inexpensive process. The easement will typically require a survey of the route. This is often skipped, but the more deals I'm involved in as a buyer and a broker, the more I opt to survey and the more I recommend a survey to my clients.

   The cost charged by the owner of the land being crossed can vary from free to what seems like a fortune. We've seen both and most things in between. This cost is usually negotiated. However, timber companies we deal with have set rates that they charge for every access they grant. Several recent deals we were able to make with two mid-sized timber companies in East Texas were structured like this: the client pays for the survey, liability insurance coverage for all who use the road, a flat administrative fee of $5000. There was also a third fee of $1.60-$3.20 per foot for the length of the easement. For the four most recent easements we secured, total costs amounted to $8000-$9000 each. That may seem like a lot until you divide that by the number of acres that now have access to a public road. Those were deals compared to the value of the land without the access.

Speaking of the value of access and the cost to acquire it, trying to nickel-and-dime my way to an access in one of the missteps I made years ago ended up costing more money in the long term. You can get the full scoop in my e-book "Land Mines – Lessons to Keep Your Rural Real Estate Deals from Blowing Up" at https://www.amazon.com/Land-Mines-Lessons-Estate-Blowing-ebook/dp/B01NAQMFHF.

Some timber companies and individuals set a price per acre for the total amount of land taken in by the easement and charge a flat amount per acre surveyed.

Remember to add in the cost of clearing land and building a road if neither exists. This can include paying for any merchantable trees that have to be removed, creek or drain crossings, ditching and crowning a road so it will drain, and surfacing the road, if desired, with rock or a more all-weather surface like asphalt.

This scenario is a pain. There's no access, and you have to jump through hoops to get it, but with some negotiation, some paperwork, and a check, you can get it. The next scenario is tougher.

3. No existing legal access, and the adjoining landowners will not cooperate in granting you one. Yes, it happens. It happens regularly in our world. For any number of reasons,

some adjoining neighbors just don't want to work with you to allow an access across their property.

This is understandable in part. Heck, no one really wants someone driving through their property and spoiling seclusion and solitude or bringing in potential problems. I get it. The other side of the coin that I don't get is when the easement they would be granting would be along a boundary line or across a very short distance near a corner where it would really have no effect on them at all. I've seen situations like this where people just dug in their heels and flat-out refused – even in remote timberland where they didn't live. This, in my opinion, is ridiculous. It is their land and their right, but their refusal seems to be more out of some sort of power trip or spite than from a position of practical concern.

What do you do if an access can't be negotiated with a stubborn landowner? That depends. Here are a few ideas. You have to decide what's best for your situation.

a. Don't buy the property. Simply decide you are not willing to deal with all the hassles and troubles, and move on to something else. If you are financing your purchase, the lender may make this decision for you. Lenders typically will not finance a deal if the closing attorney cannot ensure legal access.

    This is what most land buyers will do, and this is what I typically suggest. Unless you're a seasoned buyer with experience with the next two suggestions, I say move on. Life's too short. Find something you can thoroughly enjoy without the grief.

b. Get a legal opinion regarding your rights to sue for access. I cannot speak directly to the details of this since first, I'm not an attorney, and second, the laws and details vary from state to state. I can speak to my experiences, though, and say that I have been involved with two specific tracts where the owners sued for access. One was a quick and easy process resulting in a judgement in favor of my client, granting him the access he asked for. The second time resulted in an eventual settlement with one of three adjacent owners in which my client was granted the access. This was about a year after legal action began. He would have eventually gotten the access in court, but it would have taken much longer and would have cost even more money in time and legal fees. Both of these accounts are in the e-book "Land Mines – Lessons to Keep Your Rural Real Estate Deals from Blowing Up" at https://www.amazon.com/Land-Mines-Lessons-Estate-Blowing-ebook/dp/B01NAQMFHF.

Be sure to get good legal guidance before starting down this path. A rule of thumb: plan for it to take longer and cost more than you initially think.

c. Buy the property and try to work it out later. This is a viable option depending on the type of tract it is, how much you can buy it for, and who the adjoining owners are on all sides. Typically, landlocked tracts with no deeded access eventually sell for less than what a similar tract with access would sell for. Depending on the amount of discount you could get, it may be worth your efforts to buy it and hold it. Things change over time. Maybe you can eventually negotiate a deal for that access after all or even buy the adjoining tract. I've seen that happen more than once.

Depending on the neighbors, you may be able to get a right of passage to travel across their land to access your land for personal use or for harvesting timber. Many people are just opposed to granting something permanent (deeded easement) but will work with you on a personal basis.

There is a big difference between a right of passage (or a personal servitude) and a deeded access (perpetual easement or predial servitude). A right of passage will benefit you while you own the land but will not be passed along to heirs or a new owner. Look at it as a ticket to a baseball game. That ticket will get you into this one game, but I can't use your same ticket to go to tomorrow's game. It's your ticket for your use…so to speak. I'm speaking very generally here. That's why I encourage you to get detailed legal advice for your specific situation in your state.

We have secured these rights of entry from timber companies several times to access a landlocked tract in order to manage timber. It wasn't necessary to get a permanent easement when we could just get the right to come and go as we needed in those cases.

Let's look at another major scenario.

4. **A physical road or trail, but not a deeded access.** This is confusing for some people. They have the mindset that "Hey, there's a road to the property, so what's the problem?" The problem is that the road doesn't belong to them, and the people whose land it crosses have not granted them the right to be on it.

We see this situation a lot in the timberland of the southeast. Smaller, private tracts are scattered throughout thousands of acres of industrial timberland. The timber companies have developed road systems over decades of managing commercial forests. These roads remain, and people just use them.

The upside: a landowner with 80 acres a mile off the public road can likely use the "company" roads to access his tract any time he chooses. He may even have keys to any gates the timber company erected to keep people out when the roads are wet. Hunting clubs often lease these larger industrial acreages, and they use the gates to keep traffic down during hunting seasons and to help keep the roads in decent condition.

The downside: it's not a deeded legal access. When he gets ready to sell it to you, and you are using one of the many fine lenders through the Farm Credit System (see Jarrod Sellar's chapter on financing land), they may balk at the lack of legal access. The traditional access is there for the using, but it's not a formal grant to you and your 80 acres. That makes lenders nervous.

If you are a cash buyer, or are dealing with a lender who is familiar with these type scenarios, you can buy that 80 acres and may be able to enjoy unhindered access for years to come. But research it thoroughly. We have sold many tracts just like this through RecLand and have even bought them ourselves, so I'm not afraid of this scenario.

There are many other scenarios. Issues like using oil company (or gas company) roads and right of ways, abandoned county or parish roads, or losing access due to non-use are not uncommon. The takeaway for most buyers is to ensure that you have a perpetual, deeded access to any tract you are considering or that the tract is adjacent to a public right of way (with no gaps!). If you can't buy it with access, just pass on it and find another one. For the rest of you, carefully weigh the price and time costs of potentially obtaining an access against the possible hassles of not having a rock solid access solution before you close on the property, talk with an attorney familiar with the subject, and make your best choice.

Take a look at a short video about access at my video blog, www.RecLandTalks.com. I discuss some of the same scenarios written about here.

About the Author

Pat Porter is the broker and owner of RecLand Realty, LLC. He lives in West Monroe, Louisiana with his extremely cool boys, Hays, Joel, and Will, and his very tolerant wife, Elizabeth. Pat can be reached by email at patlporter@bellsouth.net and his main websites www.RecLand.net and www.RecLandTalks.com. Yes, he's on Facebook, Twitter, and Instagram, too. Just search for RecLand Realty.

Chapter 4 - Buying Land in the American West

By Ed Roberson, Ranch Broker at Mirr Ranch Group

Back in 2005, when I left the East Coast and moved out West to become a Rocky Mountain ranch broker, I thought I had a solid grip on the land and real estate business. I had worked for years at a well-regarded commercial real estate firm brokering the sale of all types of raw land, buildings, and warehouses. My father owned a productive farm and some timberland that was teeming with whitetails, so I was familiar with rural tracts of land with recreational value. It wasn't until after I had moved to Jackson Hole, earned my Wyoming real estate license, and started my dream job as a ranch broker that I realized all my East Coast real estate experience amounted to next to nothing in the western ranch market.

Everything about land in the West was drastically different. The landscapes were dry and arid. The topography was jagged and raw. The fish and animals were bigger, the weather was harsher, and the cowboy credo of "rugged individualism" was completely new to me. There were issues surrounding the ranch real estate market that I knew nothing about: water rights, public land leases, townships and sections, AUMs, fencing statutes, tax benefits of large-scale conservation easements, complex big game hunting regulations...the list could go on. It was as if I had landed in a foreign country.

With the help of some knowledgeable and patient mentors, a great deal of reading and study, and a healthy volume of interesting transactions (this happened to be at the height of the real estate boom), I slowly but surely began to understand the western ranch real estate market. But even now, 12 years later, I still find myself learning new aspects of the ranch real estate business, and I look forward to expanding my knowledge in the decades to come. The complexity of western ranch brokerage is precisely what makes it such an interesting and rewarding business, and also what creates opportunities for significant financial returns.

To save you some of the headaches and frustrations that I suffered during my early days of learning the ranch brokerage business, I will present several mostly western-specific issues to consider when you begin your ranch search.

Valuation

Rocky Mountain ranches are notoriously difficult to value for the following reasons:

1. Every ranch is unique.
2. There is a low volume of comparable transactions.
3. They rarely generate significant cash flow relative to value.
4. Emotion plays a notoriously large role in many transactions.

By any standard, it is an inefficient, fragmented market. But because appreciation will constitute the majority of a buyer's financial return, it is extremely important not to overpay.

It is imperative that you or your broker perform thorough research to quantitatively understand the overall land values in your area of interest, and then work hard to drill down to the value of each property. Depending on the state, this process can involve talking with banks, appraisers, and local landowners as well as digging into county records to uncover comparable sales and other useful data. There is no central database of ranch transactions as there is with commercial and residential real estate, so the process can be lengthy and time-consuming.

But in the end, having a full understanding of land values will give you a distinct advantage over landowners whose ranches are overpriced, as well as over the occasional landowner who is ignorant of market conditions and has priced a ranch well below market value. Either way, research and data are essential for identifying lucrative ranch deals.

For a more detailed analysis of ranch valuation, read my article *Valuing One-of-a-Kind Legacy Ranches* at https://www.landthink.com/valuing-one-of-a-kind-legacy-ranches/.

Water Rights

If you are from the East Coast, the idea of water rights is likely an unfamiliar concept. Water rights are an enormously complex subject, but the basic idea is that people must own (i.e., have title to) any water they divert from rivers, streams, or creeks or extract from aquifers for irrigation or storage (i.e., lakes, ponds). Laws regarding water rights can vary widely from state to state, but given the relatively small amount of rainfall in the West, high-quality water rights significantly increase the value of ranches.

Just because a creek or river runs through a property does not mean the landowner automatically owns the water rights. While you may be allowed to fish or have livestock drink from the creek, you cannot legally divert the water to irrigate or build a pond without a specific, deeded property right. Additionally, owning a water right does not necessarily mean you can irrigate your meadows freely – depending on the right's priority date, you may be forced by the state to curtail your water usage during dry years.

Because of the complexity of water rights and their ability to significantly influence the value of a ranch, it is important that you fully understand all aspects of the water rights associated with a potential ranch purchase.

1. Examine the historical usage: Many states have "use it or lose it" laws requiring that landowners use their water regularly or risk having the rights classified as "abandoned."

2. Understand the priority dates: Know when you can expect to have your water use curtailed by the state and how that will affect the ranch's agricultural operations.

3. Research the water right values: To truly appreciate the investment potential of a ranch, you must understand the specific dollar amounts that water rights or their resulting irrigated meadows and/or water features will add to the property.

In the end, water rights can be confusing to even the most seasoned experts. Dozens of books have been written on the topic, yet it can still be a difficult subject to understand. It is vital that you or your broker have a relationship with a well-regarded water rights attorney who can examine the viability of a property's water rights prior to purchase.

For more about water in the West, specifically Colorado, read my article *Water on Colorado Ranches: Four Basic Definitions* at https://www.mirrranchgroup.com/water-on-colorado-ranches-for-sale/.

Public Lands

Western states boast a staggering amount of public lands. The enormous size of Rocky Mountain states, as well as the high percentage of public versus private lands, make public lands an important issue in any large acreage rural real estate transaction. Over the course of my career, I have worked with properties that adjoin or are surrounded by public lands controlled by multiple agencies including the National Forest Service, Bureau of Land Management, National Park Service, and Bureau of Reclamation.

Whether you are buying a ranch for agricultural, recreational, or investment purposes, you must understand how any adjoining or nearby public land will affect your property. Two examples for your consideration:

1. It is common for ranches located on the lower flanks of mountain ranges to be bisected by public roads allowing access through the private property to national forest lands. Can you live with the idea of public traffic driving through your ranch on a regular basis?

2. If you are purchasing a ranch for grazing cattle, you could significantly expand your operation if you hold the grazing lease on adjacent public lands. However, in many instances these leases are tightly held by the same families for generations, making them very difficult to secure. Even if you are able to secure the lease, you must familiarize yourself with the number of animals that are allowed in your allotment and for what period of time under the terms of the lease.

Many view adjoining public lands as a way to expand their usable acreage for recreation –hunting, fishing, hiking, ATV-ing, horseback riding, etc. – without having to actually purchase deeded land. For example, if you purchase 500 acres adjoining 100,000 acres of national forest, you have direct and "free" access to huge amounts of land for recreation.

While this line of thinking is true in theory, it is important to gather local knowledge about the public land immediately adjoining your future ranch to understand how much traffic it typically receives from the public. If the public land is a popular local attraction for hunting, camping, or other recreational activities, you could potentially be facing trespassers, overcrowding during hunting season, or excessive pressure on nearby public trout streams.

Like the valuation and water rights discussed above, it is important that you or your broker immerse yourself in the details of the specific public lands that adjoin the ranches you are considering in order to make wise decisions and enjoy your future ranch to the fullest.

I could easily expand each of these three topics into its own book, so it is fair to say that I am barely scratching the surface. The more you scratch, the more you realize how complex these issues are and how they can drastically affect ranch values and your enjoyment of the property. Ranch real estate is a completely unique sector of the real estate market, so work hard or team up with a consummate professional to educate yourself prior to your investment in a Rocky Mountain ranch.

For specific instructions on how to efficiently research and understand land owned by the Bureau of Land Management, read my article *How-To: Researching BLM Master Title Plats* at https://www.mirrranchgroup.com/researching-blm-master-title-plats-on-ranches-for-sale/.

About the Author

Ed Roberson's career includes an extensive background in western ranch brokerage, commercial brokerage, and real estate development. Since moving out West in 2005, Ed has successfully brokered the sale of legacy ranches throughout Colorado, Wyoming, Montana, and Idaho, with a diverse client list that includes multi-generational ranching families, Fortune 500 companies, private equity funds, and ski resorts.

A devoted supporter of western land conservation, Ed serves as an advisor and committee member to several national and Colorado-based land trusts, and he has been a featured speaker and panelist at Colorado's annual conservation conference. He also works as an independent land conservation consultant, working on behalf of land trusts to manage the placement of conservation easements and the issuance of subsequent tax credits. Ed can be contacted at these sites: www.mirrranchgroup.com and www.mountainandprairie.com.

Chapter 5 - The Basics of Financing Unimproved Land

By Jarrod Sellar – Louisiana Land Bank, ACA

Land is a very valuable commodity, because they definitely aren't making any more of it! When I refer to land throughout this chapter, I am referring to unimproved, bare land such as row crop farm land, pasture land, timberland, etc. As an agricultural lender, I am going to concentrate on tips and information that will assist you as the buyer when planning to finance the purchase of your land. I will also touch on things every person buying land needs to do, whether you finance a portion of the purchase or not.

Purchasing a piece of property to call your own is an exciting and often life-changing event. You need to be well prepared before you step out and make that purchase.

Here are a few things I tell my customers and potential customers to do prior to purchasing their land.

1. Know where you stand financially. This is important for everyone, but especially important for you if you plan to finance land. The last thing you want to do is sit in your banker's office going over your financial information and realize that you really cannot afford to purchase the property you have your heart set on buying.

2. Meet with your banker prior to making an offer to purchase land. Sit down with your banker and tell him or her about the property you have in mind. Bring copies of your

historical income information (tax returns, W-2s, pay stubs, etc.) and personal financial statement or balance sheet. If you do not have a financial statement, sit down with your banker and create one. This will let you know where stand financially if you don't already know. Numbers 1 and 2 go hand in hand.

Take a look at our basic loan application at https://www.louisianalandbank.com/apply-for-loan to see what would be required to begin the formal loan process with us. Every lender would require an application and financial information of some sort that would likely be similar to these. You can see a financial statement form, too, that any lender would require.

3. Research the land you are looking to purchase as well as similar types of property. The best way to do this is to talk to real estate professionals like those at RecLand Realty or other land brokers in your particular region of the country. Land brokers are some of the most knowledgeable sources for this kind of information. You can also search the internet for information and check legal news for the parish or county where the land is located.

4. Be realistic and provide room for the unknown. Be realistic when making projections for cash flow or income from the property you are looking to purchase. A good example would be projecting farm rents. If you know that farms in the area where you are purchasing are renting out for an average of $125 per acre, do not run your numbers at $200 per acre just because you think you can get that for the farm. Also, be sure to leave some room in your budgeting for the unknown, such as improvements or unexpected costs you may incur. I recommend adding 5%-10% to your

budgeted expenses to provide a cushion for the unknown. If these unexpected expenses never occur, then you simply have more income to go toward your next property.

5. Know what you can afford. After you have reviewed your financial information, met with your banker, and performed research on the type of land you are looking for, you should have a good idea of what kind of down payment and loan payments you can afford.

    Use our financial calculator for a quick way to get an idea of what your loan payments would be. It's easy to plug in your information at https://www.louisianalandbank.com/products-and-services/loan-calculator.

    If you are not in the financial position at the time to make the land purchase, STOP. The last thing you need to do is overextend yourself financially, potentially losing the land you worked so hard to buy. The right time will come for you to purchase a tract of land, and if that time is not now, then you know what you need to do to get to the point where you are ready. A good financial professional like a loan officer at the Louisiana Land Bank will assist you in all of the above steps and provide you with the best advice for moving forward.

6. Research the programs that might be available for the land you are purchasing. Go to the parish or county FSA/USDA offices (this is the Farm Service Agency as part of the US Department of Agriculture) to see if there are any federal or state programs available for the type of land you are purchasing. These programs could offer an income source or other financial benefit from the land that you might not

have known was available. Some of these programs include CRP, WRE, wildlife easements, tax credits, etc. There are also programs that provide cost sharing for the expenses incurred to improve your property. These programs can be put into place after you have purchased your land. You can review the FSA website to find state offices and available programs by going to https://www.fsa.usda.gov/. Other conservation programs offered by the NRCS (Natural Resources Conservation Service), also part of the USDA, can be found at https://www.nrcs.usda.gov/wps/portal/nrcs/site/national/home/.

If you do the things listed above before you commit to purchasing a piece of land, you will be in a much better position to make that purchase. I deal with people on a daily basis who are in the process of purchasing land or wanting to purchase land. Some of them are experienced land buyers. Others are first-timers. I learned the points I have listed here from experienced land owners and professional loan officers I work hand in hand with across the state at Louisiana Land Bank. These steps are not the only things you can do before financing land, but if you take the time to do your homework on a piece of property and understand where you are financially, you will be way ahead of the game.

Here are a few other things to be keep in mind when you are financing a land purchase.

1. Understand that there will be additional out-of-pocket costs other than the down payment for financing land. Some of these costs include appraisal fees, bank fees, and attorney's closing costs. There could also be insurance requirements for the land depending on improvements that may be located on the property such as houses, barns, sheds, etc.

These "part of the process" costs could add several thousand dollars to the amount of cash you would need to have to be able to swing your deal.

2. There will be costs for the upkeep and maintenance of your new property. Some people think that after they buy the land all they have to do is pay the note. Like any investment, you need to monitor it and keep it in the possible best shape in order for it to appreciate or reach its full income-producing capacity. Whether it is mowing or bush hogging, cutting or replanting timber, controlled prescribed burning, leveling crop land, improving roads, or drilling an irrigation well to help produce higher yields on a farm, hard work will need to be done from time to time to get the most out of your property. These things will require your ability to put your hands on some cash. Some of the USDA programs referred to earlier might help with the costs of these types of projects.

3. Talk to your CPA or tax professional about your land. There are often things that can be done by your CPA with regard to taxes that can help you receive more benefit from your land. This is not always the case, but it would definitely be worth your while to check. One of the things your CPA might suggest is to form a Limited Liability Company (LLC) to purchase and own your land. This has several potential advantages, such as providing an extra layer of liability protection between you and the property as well as possibly allowing you to deduct expenses associated with the land, such as interest expense. Another possibility might be including a Schedule F in your personal tax return, which would also allow you to deduct expenses tied to the land. The point here is to get some additional information from a tax professional.

While every land transaction is unique, my goal here has been to provide you with a solid foundation to help you begin the process. Hopefully, the information provided in this chapter has provided you with a few helpful tips before you purchase and finance a tract of land.

If you ever have any questions about buying and financing land, please do not hesitate to contact me or any loan officer at your statewide Louisiana Land Bank or any bank that is part of the broader Farm Credit System. The Louisiana Land Bank website is www.louisianalandbank.com, and the site for the Farm Credit Network is https://www.farmcreditnetwork.com/.

About the Author

Jarrod Sellar is a Senior Loan Officer for Louisiana Land Bank, ACA (LLB) in their Monroe branch. He and his wife Meghan live in Jarrod's hometown of West Monroe, Louisiana. Jarrod received his Bachelor of Science degree in business management from Louisiana State University in 2007 and his Master of Business Administration (MBA) degree in 2009 from The University of Louisiana at Monroe. Jarrod has been with Louisiana Land Bank, ACA since he was hired as the company's first Credit Analyst in 2010. Jarrod was made a Loan Officer in 2013 and uses the skills he learned from his strong credit background on a daily basis. In 2016, Jarrod received his diploma from The Graduate School of Banking at LSU, where he furthered his knowledge of the complex banking industry. Jarrod can assist you with all of your agricultural financing needs, including land, equipment, and loans for operating. Please contact Jarrod by phone at 318-387-0636, by email at jarrod.sellar@louisianalandbank.com, or visit www.louisianalandbank.com.

Chapter 6 - Should You Get a Survey?

By Pat Porter – Broker/Owner, RecLand Realty, LLC

This question is as common among land buyers as the question, "Should I buy a title policy?" The answers to either question will depend on whom you're asking. Ask a closing attorney either question and you'll likely get an unequivocal "yes". Ask a professional real estate agent and you will probably hear "Well, that's your decision, but I'd probably recommend it. Better ask your attorney." Ask a seasoned land buyer and you'll hear: "…depends."

Who is right? They all are. Yes, you should get a survey – and a title policy for that matter. But it's your decision. But you may not need one. There you go. Good luck!

No. I won't leave you like that. I'll give you a little guidance. I am not a surveyor, nor do I pretend to know all the correct technical jargon for all the general scenarios we'll look at here. I'm just going to talk in generalities and tell you about some of my experiences. Talk to a professional land surveyor to get the specifics for your particular situation.

Let's look at some issues related to getting a land survey so you can make the best decision for yourself.

Some general information regarding the profession of surveying:

1. It's been said that surveying is one of mankind's oldest professions. **Elements of survey date back to Stonehenge**

(2500 B.C.) and the pyramids in Egypt (2700 B.C.). God even uses survey language when describing the Promised Land to the Israelites in the Bible. See Numbers 34.

2. Surveyors are required to have a working knowledge of many subjects like geometry, physics, trigonometry, engineering, metrology, and the law. They are also required to understand and be able to use the modern tools and technologies related to GPS, GIS, and various software.

3. A number of famous men were some of the first surveyors in our nation. George Washington, Thomas Jefferson, Abraham Lincoln, and Daniel Boone are a who's who of famous early American figures who worked as surveyors.

4. Surveyors must use more than just scientific data to perform their duties well. The art of following recorded evidence and deciphering historic intent among parties long gone is just as much part of the process as knowing how to understand the dilution of precision in satellite geometry. You may not know what all that is, but trust me, it's a stark contrast between art and science!

Before we go any further, let's take a minute to get on the same page. Throughout the rest of this chapter, my references to "a survey" will primarily be referring to a boundary survey. This is important to understand upfront, because there are many different types of land surveys that can be performed which we will not get into here.

A boundary survey is, in general terms, a land survey where a legal description – or the instructions of the parties as to how they want a parcel divided – is used to find the corners and identify the boundaries of a tract. The boundaries will close (meaning the lines will all connect to form a box or other shape) and the area within that shape can be calculated, giving you the number of acres.

A boundary survey can also accurately identify the location of other surface objects within or near the boundaries. The formal documentation of surface objects can be used for legal purposes, proof of encroachment, building guidelines, etc. Some common surface objects may be existing fences, nearby buildings or structures, roads, trails, powerlines, pipelines, creeks, retaining walls…and on and on the list can go.

So to be sure we're communicating clearly, we're only talking about boundary surveys that will establish (permanently set in the ground) all the corners, give the calls (that's the distance and direction) of each boundary line, give us the total acreage, and document any surface objects that we want identified on the tract we are considering.

People who decide not to get a survey seem to use the same faulty information to justify their decision. Here are a few of the misconceptions I regularly hear:

1. A survey is too expensive.
2. The property was surveyed in the past.
3. I know where my boundaries are.
4. The fences are the lines.
5. I know the neighbors.
6. The tax assessment states how many acres there are.
7. I'm getting a title policy.

I did not provide any rebuttals to those common reasons for declining a survey for a specific reason: I wanted the impact of the entire list to hit you. With those reasons, it's understandable why it's just downright common sense not to get that survey, right?

Let's now take a look at some reasons why you should consider surveying your next tract before you purchase it. Perhaps some of the following reasons – with their brief explanations – will help you see why I called the above items "faulty."

1. **A survey confirms a description on the ground of the property that is in the public records.** When you buy a watch from me, I'll hand you the watch. When you buy a car from me, I'll give you the keys, and you can drive away in that very same car. When I sell you 80 acres, however, I'm simply giving you a deed with a written description attached. You just get a couple sheets of paper!

    The survey will display on the ground what the words on the paper really represent. I've heard older gentleman say many times "I want to know what I'm buying" when they talk about getting a survey. The boundary survey will clearly identify the tract on the ground and give an accurate calculation of the exact acres within those boundaries.

    I cannot tell you how many tracts I've personally seen that had a measurable difference in the actual surveyed acres versus the acres that were assessed in the tax records or just assumed by the current owner. A survey confirms this.

2. **A survey will identify any encroachments.** An encroachment is when a surface structure from an adjoining property – either the entire structure or just part of it – crosses the boundary line onto your tract. Well, that is the conventional

understanding of encroachment, anyway. But did you know that an encroachment can go the other direction, too? That's right! A structure on your property could be encroaching onto the neighbor's property.

Encroachments can be expensive to resolve. They can also result in legal conflicts with neighbors. Either way, encroachments can cost more to resolve in both out-of-pocket cash and time lost in conflict than the original survey would have cost.

3. A survey will identify any easements that are on the property. Powerline and pipeline right-of-ways are common on rural tracts. The survey will also identify the actual edge of that road right-of-way, too. It's likely much wider than the actual surface of the road that runs along the edge of the property. In fact, I've seen it extend considerably further into the property than imagined on some rural highways. It's good to know this before you cut timber, build a fence or gate, or make other expensive decisions.

4. A survey will confirm legal access. We discussed this some in my chapter about access scenarios, but it is worth a reminder. Knowing precisely where your property adjoins a public road or where a deeded access connects the property to a public road is critical. The survey will clearly identify the access, or lack thereof, and will define precisely where your right of access is to be. Access roads can change over time on rural tracts. Timber company roads can shift over time. Just like the survey will help you "know what you're buying" with regard to the boundaries and acres, it will cement your access, too.

5. A survey is necessary if you plan to develop and accurately divide a tract. Creating any smaller subdivisions within a

larger parcel you plan to buy requires a boundary survey in order to be accurate in both location and size. Even if you plan to divide a square forty-acre tract into two twenties, you need a survey to determine exactly where the middle line and its two corners will be. And do you know for sure that your "40" is really 40 acres in the first place?

6. You will need a land survey to get the full benefits of your title policy coverage. I will not get into pages of legal mumbo jumbo about the exclusions and exceptions within various title policies. I will say, however, that the reason I put this point in can be summed up in one common catchall sentence from a title policy I have seen a number of times. I will put their short paragraph in my own words to avoid any issues with this nationally known title insurer: "The owner is provided <u>no coverage</u> for any matters that a survey would have likely shown."

7. Old surveys are likely not as accurate as new surveys. I know I could be picking a fight with this one. There are surveyors who come from several generations of surveyors who will fight to the death over their great granddad's dedication to and accuracy within his profession.

    I have no doubt about great granddad's dedication. He surveyed land on foot and horseback, slept under the stars for weeks on end, and traversed some rough and rugged country to do his job. We're grateful for the service he provided to our fledgling nation. He was likely as meticulous in his measurements and field notes as was humanly possible.

    But he didn't have the benefit of the Real Time Kinematic satellite navigation technique to enhance the precision of position data derived from satellite-based positioning systems. Now I'm not sure exactly what that is, but I know great granddad didn't have it. And because he didn't have it, the surveys he performed 90 years ago are likely not going to be as precise as the ones his great grandson will do today. And that 6-inch elm tree he called out as a corner blew down in a rough storm 40 years ago.

I recently signed a contract on a 60-acre tract in Texas that had legal descriptions based on 90-year-old surveys and 6-inch elm trees. I didn't hesitate to write the contract up to include a new boundary survey at our expense. It will be worth the few thousand dollars to get a modern survey to describe that tract.

8. **A survey will shed light on any existing fences.** Many rural land tracts will have fences, or partial fencing, along some or all of the boundary lines. It's very common. Chances are, those fences were used as the boundary lines in the past. In light of what we said about great granddad's technology limitations in number seven above, how accurate do you think those old fence lines might be in relation to the actual boundary? Right.

A boundary survey will let you know if the fences are encroaching onto the tract you're looking to buy, or if they're several feet away from the boundary, creating a scenario where you could have some future rights to additional acreage by prolonged possession.

Possession of acreage not acquired in good faith with a deed is called adverse possession. It's a very interesting legal situation. We cannot get into it here, but an article written by a large survey company servicing the Southeast and Mid-Atlantic States will break the concept down for you if you want to learn more: https://www.pointtopointsurvey.com/2016/07/adverse-possession-law/.

9. Get a survey if you plan to build on the tract. If your plans include building a house, shed, pond, fence, wall, pool, road, or miniature goat pen anywhere near the property line, a survey will give you the assurance you will not be encroaching on a neighbor. This applies more with smaller tracts or lots where it could be easy to cross the line. I have an attorney friend who sums it up like this: "As civilization gets closer, precision matters." Well said.

10. Get a survey to document what is on the ground. Look at it like this: a survey provides an official and detailed snapshot of what the tract looked like and the precise location of all the surface objects that were on or near it at a precise point in time.

    Not long ago, I had the area surveyed where an access was to cross a small portion of ground and connect our tract with a public road. The area in question was less than the size of half a basketball court. But that survey provided much more information than the acreage of the land. It documented precisely where a gas meter was located, where a neighbor's driveway was, called out several electric poles, showed where the public road surface ended, and depicted the road's entire right-of-way. It pointed out the width of a culvert and how far it was located from the edge of the access and the edge of the public road. It detailed many other items, but I'll stop the list now to keep you from dozing off.

The survey was not so much to help me know where our access was to be. Its real purpose was to document, with precision, where all those other items were in relation to our land and the access. We were having some problems getting the supervising authority to approve a subdivision, and all these items in and near our access point were potential issues at the time. With the survey, I had an official "snapshot" of what was on the ground if a judge ever needed to know the facts about that situation.

11. Get a survey if you want to buy by the acre. Seems pretty simple, but people get crossed up on this one all the time. There are two ways you will buy a tract of land: A total, lump sum purchase or a per-acre purchase.

    What's the difference? A lump sum purchase is just that – you are paying a specific sum of money for the property described. The exact acreage is not really a factor. If I tell you I'll give you $80,000 for the property you're calling a 40-acre tract, then I'm just giving you $80,000 regardless of whether it is really 37 acres or 42 acres. We're calling it 40 acres. It has a legal description. We make the deal, and it's done.

    If, however, I tell you that I'll give you $2000 per acre, you may assume you're getting $80,000. But after the survey shows it's 38.75 acres, you will have a final purchase price of $77,500. Now, a good land agent will get all this clearly defined in the purchase agreement so there is no confusion. But as a buyer, you need to know what you're buying and how the final purchase may be adjusted or how you may end up with more or less acres than you thought if the property is ever surveyed in the future. People usually learn this lesson when they get ready to sell that 40 acres, and the new buyer has it surveyed. Only then will you learn that you were "shorted" over an acre. But you weren't shorted if you bought it for an $80,000 lump sum. You just assumed the acreage instead of getting a survey.

The 1.25 acres in this example is not all that big a deal. But if you purchased 47 parcels in a large timberland package of many thousands of acres like our investment group recently did, then shortages in acres can be an expensive issue.

I'm sure there are lots of other reasons to get a boundary survey. There a certainly many more reasons you'd need different types of surveys. But we will stop here. These 11 reasons will cover most of the major scenarios as to why you really should get that survey before you close on a property.

Would you assume that I get a survey on all or most of the tracts I am personally involved in buying? Those 11 solid reasons could lead you to believe I always do. Well, I do get surveys more often now than not. I rarely used to get a survey. Now I rarely decline a survey. I have gotten to the point that the peace of mind and "knowing what I'm buying" makes it much easier to justify those few thousand dollars in extra cost. But even with that, I don't always get a survey.

Here are a few general reasons I may elect to pass on the survey:

1. **There was a recent survey.** If the current owner had a survey done within the last several years, I usually don't get a new one.

2. **It's a well-marked timberland tract** adjoining other timberland tracts. We have both bought and helped facilitate the sale of thousands of acres of timberland and recreational tracts. These tracts were typically bought from large timber companies that were diligent in maintaining

their boundary lines and had done so for decades. There were monuments (permanent markers) at the corners and paint on the trees on the boundary lines. These lines are pretty solid and almost fool-proof. You can put a lot of confidence in them.

3. The property adjoins state or federal land. Usually, these boundary lines are established to a high degree of certainty. I am pretty comfortable with them.

4. The aerial imagery maps out to the correct acreage. This is not a foolproof way to determine acreage. In fact, I don't recommend you put any degree of confidence in mapping a tract out on any of today's aerial imagery software unless you have been doing this for a long time. This is more art than science. Once you've seen as many tracts as guys like us see and have mapped thousands of tracts using several different versions of software, I'd take the humble position here and assume you can't count on it. You have to often make educated assumptions as to boundary lines based on timber type changes, old roads along section or quarter section lines, and a whole host of other "clues" to get it close. I would never do this on a 1.15-acre lot in a subdivision. I do rely on this more often than not on a 200-acre recreational tract, though.

Let me give you a few tips to help you get the most out of your survey:

1. Always get a plat. The surveyor has done all the field work necessary to set all the corners and write a legal description narrative that can be used for the deed and to calculate the acres. Go ahead and spend the extra couple hundred bucks

for a color plat with the tract overlaid on aerial imagery. The visual representation is useful as well as just nice to have. You are truly seeing what you're buying.

2. Identify any existing monuments on the tract ahead of time. If you are able to do a little legwork in advance of the surveyor getting on the scene, then you may save some money by saving him some time. I routinely do this where I can and put fresh flagging on all existing monuments to help him find them. I use a machete and cut away all the brush so he can quickly see it and get to it. If he is stomping around, looking, and cutting brush, he is likely charging you for that time. Take a look as I discuss this on my video blog: http://www.reclandtalks.com/land-stuff/find-survey-points-on-your-land-to-save-some-money.

3. Have the surveyor mark some additional points along long boundary lines. I call this "adding some midpoints." I know they aren't really midpoints. They are just additional points along longer boundary lines that the surveyor can easily get to (like along existing trails or openings in the timber). These extra points make it easier to identify the lines between the corners and give extra check points for someone to flag and paint your boundary lines. See the video about flagging in lines yourself on our blog: http://www.reclandtalks.com/land-stuff/flagging-boundary-lines-on-timber-land.

   I talk more about these midpoints and how they are very handy on larger recreational tracts in a very informative video on our blog: http://www.reclandtalks.com/land-stuff/ideas-to-maximize-a-land-survey-when-marking-boundary-lines-on-rural-land-tracts.

4. Mark the lines yourself. Use the information in number three above, watch the videos, and decide if you feel comfortable marking the lines between the corners yourself. You could also have a forester do it. This will be cheaper than having the surveyor blaze your lines on larger tracts.

   I only recommend this on timberland and recreational tracts where you don't need a dead straight, adjusted for declination, right-on-the-money line marked. You just need a visible line along the boundary that will help you and your neighbors know where you are. If you decide to do this, you'll be glad you watched the videos and had those extra midpoints put in!

5. Try to use the same surveyor if possible. If you find yourself doing more than one deal, you'll end up developing a good relationship that can save you money, time, and grief going forward. Learn from him. If he gains your trust, lean on him during the awkward deals and listen to what he recommends. He has likely seen more situations than you and may be able to point out the booby traps.

Whether or not you get a survey when your lender isn't demanding one and you don't need one to legally describe the tract for the closing attorney is entirely your call. If I had to make one blanket statement to all buyers for all time, I'd say to get the survey. You and I know, however, that we can make good deals without the surveyor. But at the end of the day...I'm likely going to call him.

About the Author

Pat Porter is the broker and owner of RecLand Realty, LLC. He lives in West Monroe, Louisiana with his extremely cool boys, Hays, Joel, and Will, and his very tolerant wife, Elizabeth. Pat can be reached by email at patlporter@bellsouth.net and his main websites www.RecLand.net and www.RecLandTalks.com. Yes, he's on

Facebook, Twitter, and Instagram, too. Just search for RecLand Realty.

Wrapping It All Up

Thanks for reading my humble little book.

I hope you got an idea or two that will help you in your next land deal. The information provided here is the real deal. The contributors are in this business and deal with these issues – and many more – on a daily basis.

There may have been other topics you wanted to see discussed, and I get that. There are so many specific topics that can be covered since there is such a vast variety of land types, sizes, and uses all over our great country. We will keep trying to provide more information in new books and videos as we go.

Please take a minute to provide a review of my book. It just takes a second, and they are so valuable to us writers trying to make our material available to people online. I believe you got plenty of value for the cost in this deal, so I would be grateful for your help in giving this book a little notice so it can be useful to others, too.

At RecLand Realty, all we do is land. Let us know when we can serve you. We can be found pretty easily at www.RecLand.net or on one of our sister sites like www.landforsalevideos.net.

Our video blogs are at www.RecLandTalks.com and www.LandInfoSite.com. At these blogs, you will see dozens of short videos where I discuss land-related subjects as well as things associated with the RecLand brand. You'll read short summaries about products we use, resources we can recommend, and just about whatever we want to discuss about land and the outdoors.

You can learn a lot of specific details about rural land there. Take a look at them and use the tags on each page to help you locate the videos and subjects you have interest in.

You can also find out what we're up to at www.facebook.com/recland and www.twitter.com/reclandrealty. We have several other Twitter and Facebook pages, as well as an Instagram account related to the RecLand brand. Just search RecLand or RecLand Realty and join us. I am always accessible by email at patlporter@bellsouth.net.

Remember, this information is provided as-is and does not in any way make or imply any guarantees as to any outcome. You will need to evaluate the information herein and consult the appropriate professionals such as surveyors, attorneys, tax accountants, or any other professional or agency to acquire the information and guidance you need to help you make the decision that is best for you.

Pat Porter, Broker

RecLand Realty, LLC – 410 Olive Street – Monroe, LA 71201

Other land and real estate books by Pat Porter:

"How to Sell Your Land Faster – Proven Ways to Improve the Value & Desirability of Rural Land" is available in e-book, paperback & audio at Amazon at https://www.amazon.com/How-Sell-Your-Land-Faster-ebook/dp/B01GU6NF4A.

"The Stuff the Best Land Agents Do: And You Should Do Them, Too!" is available in e-book & audio at Amazon at https://www.amazon.com/Stuff-Best-Land-Agents-Do-ebook/dp/B01JVET6NM.

"Land Buying Tips from the Pros – How to Buy Rural Real Estate" is available in e-book, paperback & audio at Amazon at https://www.amazon.com/Land-Buying-Tips-Pros-Estate-ebook/dp/B01M13FQRS.

"Land Mines: Lessons to Keep Your Rural Real Estate Deals from Blowing Up" is available in e-book & audio at Amazon at https://www.amazon.com/Land-Mines-Lessons-Estate-Blowing-ebook/dp/B01NAQMFHF.

"Dumb Questions: Avoid Asking These Questions When You Are Buying Rural Real Estate" is available in e-book & audio at Amazon at https://www.amazon.com/Dumb-Questions-asking-questions-estate-ebook/dp/B06WW5D9TD.

Or just visit my author page at https://www.amazon.com/Pat-Porter/e/B00LWUVMS6 to see them all in one place.

Bonus Chapter

Due Diligence – Some Additional Items to Check before Buying Rural Land

By Pat Porter

From "Land Buying Tips from the Pros – How to Buy Rural Real Estate" available in e-book, paperback & audio at Amazon at https://www.amazon.com/Land-Buying-Tips-Pros-Estate-ebook/dp/B01M13FQRS.

I looked up the definition of due diligence in several places and found these recurring words: investigation, analysis, research, reasonable, certainty, and confirmation. These are heavy words that carry a lot of responsibility. And all this responsibility falls squarely on the shoulders of you, the buyer, when you plan to buy land.

No one will care about the details of the deal any more than you. Doing your due diligence can save you a lot of future heartache and money on that land tract you're about to buy. In this short chapter, I'll outline several key areas, in addition to the things most people check when buying real estate, that will get you thinking about what else to check and verify during your next rural real estate purchase.

The Purchase Contract

Due diligence starts with the purchase contract. Read it, understand it, ask questions about it, and use it to fully detail the terms of the purchase as they have been negotiated with the seller. Your land agent should be diligent in helping you document the terms of the deal clearly in the purchase contract. Having the seller and buyer see "eye to eye" on the terms at this stage of the deal will reduce the chances of something going wrong for either party before closing. Regardless of how well things seem to be going at this stage, get all the verbal agreements written into the contract. Even the best of intentions can fall prey to bad memories and misunderstandings later on.

Remember, a purchase contract by its design will capture all the big items in a deal that rarely cause the problems. Things like purchase price, closing date, and legal description won't usually be an issue later on. It's the smaller things that creep up and bugger up a deal (yea, "bugger up" is a highly technical real estate term). Get those smaller details on paper at the beginning.

Existing Easements & Leases

Depending on the present use of the land, you will need to verify a number of items that will affect your future use of the tract. Have you seen the CRP or WRP contracts that are still in place on the tract? Have you read the restrictions of the conservation easement, the deed restrictions, timber reservations, or other encumbrances that will limit the use of the tract? Have you or your attorney actually seen and read them? What about that hunting lease or farm lease…does it match what you were told during the negotiating process? Ask to see the conveyance document on "deeded accesses" if you are depending on it for your supposed legal access.

All the above contracts and leases are available either as recorded documents in your county or parish records (these are public information), the local Farm Service Agency (you'll need the landowner's permission to get copies here), or from the current owner. Be sure your written purchase agreement has language that says the seller has provided you with a copy of any lease, easement, or agreement that may not be found in the public records.

Here's an example of how this type of follow-up saved a large acreage deal. I was helping a group of buyers purchase nearly 2000 acres of bottomland that was a purely recreational tract. They knew they weren't getting the mineral rights since those rights were already under lease, and the tract had a number of producing gas wells on it. They were concerned, however, that all the coming and going of the gas company would be a problem for them when trying to divide the tract and sell parcels to hunters. After all, who wants to spend a bunch of money on a place to deer hunt and then have people riding through your property at 9 a.m. checking a gas well?

I found out who the gas company was and made a call. I was able to speak with the field supervisor for that area and that tract. He told me they had a policy about limiting property visits during hunting season and that they try to come only during the middle of the day when it was necessary.

This piece of information eased the buyers' minds, and they bought the tract. Their resell efforts were also successful, since this little bit of information was enough to make the original concern a nonissue. But they wouldn't have known without the additional phone call. And it's the kind of phone call and follow-up that isn't part of the closing attorney's general checklist of things to do. You have to do this kind of checking for yourself.

Wetlands

If you plan to clear some of the tract for farming, development, or even a new road, will you be clearing wetlands? You don't know until you've seen a wetland determination report. Will that bridge you need require a 404 Permit from the Corps of Engineers or expensive mitigation credits?

Go to the Corps website at www.usace.army.mil and click on the "Find a Corp Office" link to get the office in your area. You'll find there are 30-40 offices in the United States, with most of them located in the eastern half of the country. Call and ask if you're not certain.

"But Pat, I'll be opening up a can of worms if I call them!" I hear you…and tend to agree a little bit. But you could be opening a can of snakes – in the form of expensive litigation and after-the-fact remedies – if you don't check before you begin an expensive, or expansive project. Our experience has shown that these folks will guide you to perform only what's necessary as your project impacts wetlands, streams, etc. and leave you alone if your plans don't otherwise cross into this type of problem area.

If in doubt…call them before you buy.

Environmental Issues

Diligent buyers of farmland look for large diesel spills at wells and near full tanks and check for empty chemical containers dumped in nearby ditches or creeks to alert them of potential environmental quality issues. A Phase 1 environmental evaluation is not a big deal to get, but it could turn into a big deal if you don't.

You can get good information about this from your state's Department of Environmental Quality. Simply Google "Department of Environmental Quality" to find your state's particular website. They can direct you to local companies or consultants who can perform these checks for you.

Timber Markets

Timberland buyers should understand the area markets and mills if buying a tract in a new area. How far away are the area mills, and what type of wood product are they taking? Will the terrain allow complete mechanical harvest, or are there acres that loggers just won't be able to work? This can be costly to find out later if you placed a considerable value on the timber in those unworkable areas. Do you have good access to get your timber out? Not all timber markets are the same. Not all timber tracts are the same, either. Consulting a local forester in an area you're new to may prevent a costly mistake.

Title, Mineral and Groundwater Checks

Your closing attorney should be able to catch title issues that may cause you problems if left unresolved, but you may need to specify that he look for items that are critical to your reason for purchase. For instance, if you're buying half the mineral rights, does that mean half of 100%, or does the seller only own 50% herself and you're really just getting half of half? A general title search will not necessarily determine this information for you. If confirming this information is critical, you'll need to take the initiative to have a mineral abstract performed.

A word of caution about title searches: It could be helpful to you to be sure your attorney checks the title back further than a typical "30 years plus 1 chain" in order to pick up some old leases that may have been executed 40-50 years ago, or longer. These leases exist. I've seen them, and I've seen this very issue create problems for buyers and sellers. A title policy can help reduce risks associated with title issues. We have a chapter devoted to title policies in this book. It's written by a practicing attorney specializing in real estate transactions. Be sure to read it.

If you are buying land in a state like Texas where groundwater can be reserved, you will want to know the status on your tract. Be sure to ask your attorney or title company.

Flood Plains and Access to River Tracts

You can verify river stages, flood histories, and FEMA flood plain data yourself online these days if the tract is in a marginal elevation area. But you need to do this. Ask your land agent to help you identify internet resources if you need them. Confirm the information you've been told if you're unsure. Ask your homeowner's insurance agent to help you check the area where you may plan to build a home or a camp.

What river stage at the nearest upstream bridge does a rising river cut off use of the access road to your property? When was the last time it got this high...or how often does it?

Here's the best place to start if you want to investigate the federal database for floodplains in the U.S.: www.fema.gov. Click the Navigation tab on the left. Scroll down and click the Flood Map Service Center tab. This will take you to a page where you can enter the property's location, and the site will locate the flood plain map for that area. You'll see an overview of the flood zone designations. This is a good place to start, especially if you have plans to build on the property.

The list of items to verify can go on and on depending on the tract and its use. The point is to confirm, verify, and understand all the major items that will impact you the hardest. Your land agent is required by law to tell you about all material facts he is aware of that may impact the property's value and use. The key is "that he is aware of." Your agent may not know everything about every detail that is critical to you. You as the buyer are ultimately responsible to satisfy and protect your future interests, to your satisfaction and level of comfort, with thoughtful due diligence.

About the Author

Pat Porter is the broker for RecLand Realty, LLC. His main office is in Monroe, Louisiana. His company site is www.RecLand.net and its video blog is www.RecLandTalks.com. RecLand has a new blog at www.LandInfoSite.com. Feel free to email Pat at patlporter@bellsouth.net.

Thanks again! Please take a minute to see our other land-related books at https://www.amazon.com/Pat-Porter/e/B00LWUVMS6 and leave a review on Amazon for any of the books you have read.

Made in the USA
Columbia, SC
02 April 2023